Opposites
at the Park

By Kathleen Connors

Gareth Stevens
Publishing

Please visit our website, www.garethstevens.com. For a free color catalog of all our high-quality books, call toll free 1-800-542-2595 or fax 1-877-542-2596.

Library of Congress Cataloging-in-Publication Data

Connors, Kathleen.
Opposites at the park / Kathleen Connors.
    p. cm. — (Word play)
Includes index.
ISBN 978-1-4339-7192-1 (pbk.)
ISBN 978-1-4339-7193-8 (6-pack)
ISBN 978-1-4339-7191-4 (library binding)
1. English language—Synonyms and antonyms—Juvenile literature. I. Title.
PE1591.C6693 2012
428'.1—dc23
                            2011051766

First Edition

Published in 2013 by
Gareth Stevens Publishing
111 East 14th Street, Suite 349
New York, NY 10003

Copyright © 2013 Gareth Stevens Publishing

Designer: Ben Gardner
Editor: Kristen Rajczak

Photo credits: Cover, p. 1 Digital Vision/Ryan McVay/Thinkstock; p. 5 Dmitriy Shironosov/Shutterstock.com; p. 7 iofoto/Shutterstock.com; p. 9 Carlos E. Santa Maria/Shutterstock.com; p. 11 Philip Date/ Shutterstock.com; p. 13 ©iStockphoto.com/Steven Miric; p. 15 ©iStockphoto.com/Mark Tooker; p. 17 ©iStockphoto.com/Ewald Grabenbauer; p. 19 ©iStockphoto.com/Shaun Lowe.

Printed in the United States of America

CPSIA compliance information: Batch #CS12GS: For further information contact Gareth Stevens, New York, New York at 1-800-542-2595.

Contents

Boldface words appear in the glossary.

What's an Opposite?

The park is a great place to learn about opposites! Opposites are words with **meanings** that are as different as possible. Opposites are also called antonyms.

Yes and **no** are opposites. They're as different as possible!

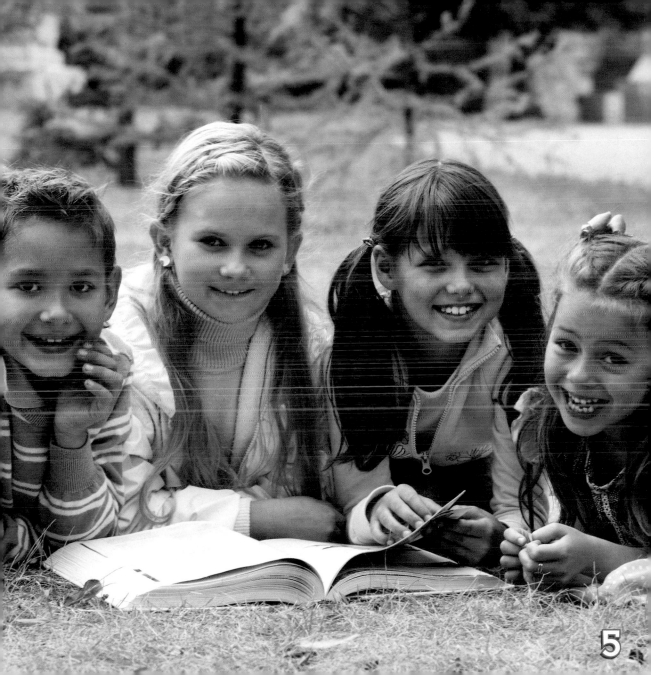

Keep Running

You have to run **fast** when you play tag at the park. If you go **slow** you'll get caught. Tag, you're it!

Fast means to move very quickly. **Slow** means the opposite! **Fast** and **slow** are antonyms.

Up, Up, and Away

Sometimes, swinging feels like flying! When you're on a swing, you start **low**. You move your legs back and forth to swing **high**.

Low and **high** are opposites. Their meanings are as different as possible.

9

Super Slides

Going **down** slides at the park is fun! To go **down** a slide, you have to climb **up** its ladder.

Do **up** and **down** mean different things? Yes! They're opposites.

In the Branches

Most parks have lots of trees for climbing or giving shade. **Old** trees are **tall**. **Young** trees are **short**.

Tall and **short** are antonyms. So are **old** and **young**!

13

Batter Up!

Do you play sports at the park? Even though one team **wins** and one team **loses**, everyone can still have fun!

Win and **lose** have meanings that are as different as possible. They're opposites!

15

Summer and Winter

You can play in the park during all kinds of weather! When it's **hot**, you can swim. When it's **cold**, you can ice-skate or build a snowman.

Hot means the **temperature** is high. **Cold** means the temperature is low. They're opposites.

Play All Day

Parks **open** during the **day** and **close** at **night**. It's important to follow each park's rules so you can play safely.

Open and **close** have opposite meanings. **Day** is the opposite of **night**. Both sets of words are antonyms.

PARK CLOSED

The Opposite of Opposite

Even the word **opposite** has an opposite! It's the word **same**.

Opposite and **same** have different meanings. They're antonyms!

Common Opposites

front	→	back
big	→	little
in	→	out
off	→	on
loud	→	quiet
wet	→	dry

Glossary

meaning: the message behind a word or words

temperature: how hot or cold something is

For More Information

Books

Jordan, Apple. *Hot Cold*. New York, NY: Marshall Cavendish Benchmark, 2012.

Phillips, Jillian. *Opposites*. London, England: Scholastic, 2012.

Websites

Learning About Opposites
www.fisher-price.com/us/fun/games/opposites
Practice more opposites in this fun game.

Quiet Quest for Opposites
www.earobics.com/gamegoo/games/squanky/squanky.html
Help Squanky find the opposites in this video and game.

Index